Lost Glory

Great Days of the American Railways

Ian Logan

H·A·R·M·O·N·Y B·O·O·K·S

New York

To Barnaby and Harriet

First published in the United States, in 1977 by Harmony Books,
a division of Crown Publishers, Inc. All rights reserved under
the International Copyright Union by Harmony Books.
Originally published by Mathews Miller Dunbar Ltd., London 1977
form or by any means, electronic or mechanical, including
photocopying, recording, or by information and retrieval
system, without permission from the Publisher.
Harmony Books
A division of Crown Publishers, Inc.
One Park Avenue
New York, New York 10016

Published simultaneously in Canada by
General Publishing Company, Limited.

Printed in England.

ISBN 0-517-530953 (cloth)

ISBN 0-517-530961 (paperback)

LOST GLORY

LOST GLORY records the heyday of the American railroads. I hope that it will stimulate interest in a period which saw what must surely have been the most exciting collection of graphic imagery ever to have been produced in this field anywhere in the world.

The American Railroad systems were privately owned. The men who ran them were tough, go-getting, enterprising. The competition between them was immense and responsible for a range and quality of graphic symbols, names and advertising, the equal of which no other industry had ever produced.

Every freight-car or carriage was quite distinct, even within the same company and I have tried to represent this by varying the images as much as possible.

From the late 30s to the early 50s, the American railroads reached their climax. Competition was at its most fierce and advertising at its peak. Already they were being threatened by air passenger travel companies who finally destroyed them. Many of the smaller railroad companies went bankrupt or were forced to merge with bigger ones. Freight-carriers became the backbone of the railroads and today the lines catering for passengers are negligible.

What passenger lines remain are in the hands of a government-based system called Amtrak which to this day run their locomotives on the same routes as all the early 'Streamliner' trains.

The names of these great locomotives still echo along the tracks: the Burlington Zephyrs, Rock Island Rockets, GM & O Rebels, Milwaukee Roads Hiawathas, Dixie Flyers, Wabash Cannonballs, and, last but not least, the Atchinson, Topeke and Santa Fe, Chieftains and El Capitans.

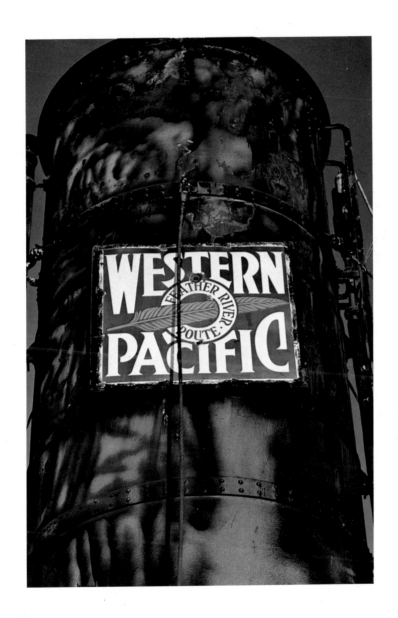

1 View from cab of Amtrak train at oncoming Union Pacific freight train near Cheyenne, Wyoming, December 1976.
2 DDA40X built to special order for Union Pacific by EMD in 1971 and named centennial type to commemorate 100th anniversary of completion of the transcontinental railroad at Promontory, Utah in 1869, photographed at Vernon Yard, L.A.
3 Safety slogan on Union Pacific Caboose, Vernon Yard, L.A.
4 Safety slogan on Union Pacific Caboose, Vernon Yard, L.A.
5 Union Pacific street advertisement in Los Angeles of DDA40X.
6 Union Pacific symbol on a freight car, Vernon Yard, L.A.
7 Union Station, L.A.
8 Interior of Union Station, L.A.
9 G.M. & O., 883A on last journey, EMD.F3, (Kansas City Rail Museum).
10 One of two Aerotrains built by EMD in 1956 and donated to the St. Louis Museum in 1966.
11 Western Pacific Caboose, built October 1943, Sacramento.
12 WP 4.8.2. Mountain type, designed by USRA and built by Alco during the 1920's. Now at the North California Railroad Museum.
13 Western Pacific freight car with giant feather slogan and 'Rides Like a Feather' motif, Kansas City South Yards, Kansas City.
14 Steam tug 'Hercules' once owned by Western Pacific for work with ferries. San Francisco Maritime Museum.
15 Funnel of steam tug 'Hercules'.
16 Santa Fe Geep, GP38, No. 2503, Long Beach, California.
17 Side view of GP38.
18 Fleet of Electro Motive Division GPs at the fuelling base, Hobart Yard, Los Angeles.
19 Atchinson, Topeke and Santa Fe freight car, built 72nd street Yard, New York.
20 ATSF Caboose, Richmond, California.
21 SP AC12 (Articulated Consolidation) 2.88.4 Oil burning, so cab forward to avoid fumes. Sacramento, California.
22 Southern Pacific railway station, San Francisco.
23 Southern Pacific symbol on workers truck, Salinas Valley, California.
24 Southern Pacific symbol on bench in Sacramento station.
25 Southern Pacific symbol on freight car, Sacramento.
26 Ad in San Francisco railway station for the 'Shasta Daylight'.
27 Interior of Southern Pacific skydome on Amtrak Train.
28 View from cab of Amtrak train near Laramie, Wyoming.
29 Illinois Central and Gulf GP9's with 'chopped noses' moving along the track in St. Louis.
30 Illinois Central & Gulf Caboose, St. Louis.
31 Illinois Central & Gulf SD 38Y with six wheel trucks, 'Eugene Stetson', St. Louis.
32 Drum Head of hospitality car, San Francisco.
33 Drum Head of Comet hospitality car, North California Railroad Museum.
34 Key System logo, North California Railroad Museum.
35 East Bay transit logo in electric tram car, North California Railroad Museum.

36 MKT logo on freight car, Vernon Yard, Los Angeles.
37 Mexican Railroad logo on freight car, Vernon Yard, Los Angeles.
38 Cast makers nameplate from steam loco, St. Louis railroad museum.
39 Frisco SD45 (20 cylinder engine – the largest ever put into a US diesel). Engine 926, Burlington Northern Yards, Kansas City.
40 Cotton Belt GP40, St. Louis.
41 Kansas City Southern Drumhead on hospitality car, Kansas City Railroad Museum.
42 Interior of Hospitality car.
43 Mopac engines in the evening, Kansas City.
44 Kansas City Southern EMD NW2, 1,000 HP switcher, Kansas City.
45 Kansas City Southern SD40's with new livery, Kansas City,
46 Canadian National logo on freight car, Kansas City,
47 British Columbia railway freight car, Kansas City.
48 Canadian Pacific car, built October 1955, Union Pacific Yards, Los Angeles.
49 Canadian Pacific freight car, built 1955, Vernon Yard, Los Angeles.
50 Canadian National logo on freight car, built January 1956, Kansas City.
51 East Bay Transit, electric interurban car by the American Car Company, North California Railroad museum.
52 Florida East Coast GP7, Miami, Florida.
53 Front view of old Burlington Zephyr, St. Louis Railroad Museum.
54 Rear view of the great Burlington Zephyr, now owned by a bank in Kansas City.
55 Burlington Freight car with old company logo, built July 1937, Vernon Yard, Los Angeles.
56 Florida East Coast with old company logo, Miami, Florida.
57 Sante Fe logo on freight car, San Francisco.
58 Burlington Northern symbol on freight car, New York.
59 Pennsylvania RR Keystone logo pre the Penn, New York Central merger into Penn Central, New York.
60 Cotton Belt symbol on freight car, Los Angeles.
61 Drum head of KCS car.
62 Symbol from Union Pacific freight car.
63 Mopack EMD SW1200 road switcher with Missouri Pacific symbol, St. Louis.
64 New Mopac eagle logo on GP40 EMD switcher, St. Louis.
65 Old MP symbol on freight car, built September 1958. Los Angeles.
66 Light consolidation 2.8.0 steam locomotive at Kansas City Railway Museum.
67 Wreck of PFE mechanical reefer in the Selinas Valley, California.
68 Sacramento Northern EMD NW2 road switcher, Sacramento, California.
69 Sacramento Northern General Electric steeplecab 50 Ton, Sacramento.
70 Northwestern Pacific Logo, San Francisco Maritime Museum.
71 Seaboard coastline EMD E6, Denver, Colorado.
72 Delaware and Hudson freight car, New York.
73 Delaware and Hudson freight car, New York.

110 Chicago and North Western Hopper, Kansas City.
111 Spokane, Portland and Seattle freight car. Built July, 1949. Kansas City.
112 Milwaukee Road freight car, built December 1966, 72nd Street Yard, New York.
113 Milwaukee Road symbol, Kansas City.
114 Atlantic Coast line symbol on Piggy Back, 72nd Street Yard, New York.
115 Chicago and Illinois symbol – steam loco, St Louis Rail Museum.
116 Wabash symbol on refrigerated box car. Kansas City.
117 View from cab of Amtrak engine.
118 View from cab of Amtrak engine in Wyoming.
119 L & N GP38 road switcher, St Louis.
120 SR & N NW1 EMD switcher, North California rail museum.
121 RD & G freight car, Miami.
122 Soo Line freight car, built July 1953. 72nd Street Yard, New York.
123 Norfolk and Western freight car, Miami.
124 Northern Pacific freight car, built March 1946. Kansas City.
125 Northern Pacific GP7 in Montana. (Photo Alan Uglow).
126 Bart Transit system, Concord Station, California.
127 View of Burlington Northern yards from control tower, Kansas City.
128 Amtrak locomotive, SDP40F, Miami.
129 Rail box freight car, Miami.
130 View towards Kansas City from Control Tower, BN Yards.

My thanks to:
James A Bryant – Amtrack
John Russell – supervisor, Union Pacific
Union Pacific Yards, Los Angeles.
Santa Fe Yards, Los Angeles and San Francisco
Charles Pitcher – Kansas City Southern
David Peironnet – Kansas City Southern
Al Krieg, Union Pacific Public Relations
Mr. Condotta – Burlington KC,
and Bernard Myers for editing my notes.